CHARLIE BROWN'S 'CYCLOPEDIA

Super Questions and Answers and Amazing Facts

Featuring
Stars and Planets
and Plants

Volume 8

Based on the Charles M. Schulz Characters

Funk & Wagnalls, Inc.

Photograph and Illustration Credits: Jen and Des Bartlett/Bruce Coleman, Inc., xi; Harold Roth, x.

3 4 5 6 7 8 9 0

A large part of the material in this volume was previously published in *Charlie Brown's Second Super Book of Questions and Answers.*

Introduction

Welcome to volume 8 of *Charlie Brown's 'Cyclopedia*! Have you ever wondered why stars twinkle, or how hot the sun is, or why leaves turn color in the fall? Charlie Brown and the rest of the *Peanuts* gang are here to help you find the answers to these questions and many more about stars, planets, and plants. Have fun!

The Stars and the Planets

What are stars?

When you look up at the sky on a clear night, you see many, many twinkling points of light. These are the stars. They are really huge balls of bright, hot, glowing gases. They pour out light, just the way the sun does. In fact, the sun *is* a star. The other stars look much smaller than the sun because they are much farther away from the earth.

What makes the stars shine?

Stars shine with their own light because they are very hot. A lot of gases press down at the center of a star to cause this great heat.

Why do stars twinkle?

Stars don't really twinkle. They just seem to. There is a thick blanket of air around the earth. The light coming from the stars must pass through this air. As the starlight passes through, it shifts, or moves about. This happens because of moisture in the air, changing air temperatures, and the constant movement of the air. To us the shifting starlight looks like twinkling.

Long, long ago, some people believed the stars were lamps hanging from a huge ceiling!

337

How many stars are there in the sky?

On a clear night, you can see about 2,000 stars just by looking up. You could see many thousands more with a small telescope. You could see billions more with a very powerful telescope. Scientists keep inventing stronger telescopes. With each new one, the scientists discover more stars. So no one really knows how many stars there are in the sky.

What does a telescope do?

A telescope makes things appear much larger than they really are. In this way it is something like a magnifying glass, but much more powerful. A telescope also makes things appear brighter than they are. When you look through a telescope, faraway things seem closer and look clearer. So for a long time people have been using telescopes for studying the stars and planets.

Today there is another kind of telescope that has nothing to do with seeing. It is called a radio telescope. It picks up movements in the air called radio waves that come from outer space. All stars and some planets give off these waves. So do other faraway objects. By listening to radio waves, scientists learn more about everything in outer space.

Will the same stars always be in the sky?

No. Old stars are always dying and new stars are always being born. Some stars last only a few million years. Others go on and on for hundreds of billions of years. But all stars either explode or get small and stop shining. At the same time, new stars keep forming from gas and dust in space.

> It takes many millions of years for light to travel from a far-off star to your eyes. So some of the stars you see in the sky really burned out long, long ago!

Where do the stars go in the daytime?

They don't go anywhere. They are always in the sky. But the sun's bright light keeps you from seeing the stars during the day. Only in the evening can you begin to see them again.

How big are stars?

Stars are the biggest single thing scientists know of. Our own sun is a star, and it is more than a million times larger than the earth. The sun is a middle-sized star, and many other stars are about its size. But some stars, called dwarfs, are much smaller—about the size of the earth. Other stars, called giants and supergiants, are much larger than the sun. The biggest supergiants known are about 500 times larger than the sun.

!

Stars come in many colors—blue, white, yellow, orange, or red!

What is the Big Dipper?

The Big Dipper is a group of bright stars in the sky. They look like the cup and handle of a water dipper. The Big Dipper is one of many groups of stars that people have named for their shapes. We call these groups constellations (kon-stuh-LAY-shunz).

MIZAR

NORTH STAR

BIG DIPPER

I THOUGHT A DOUBLE STAR MEANT PAUL NEWMAN AND ROBERT REDFORD... HA, HA, HA, HA,... YES MA'AM.

Is there such a thing as a double star?

Yes, there are thousands of them. A double star is made up of two neighboring stars that travel around each other. Mizar (MY-zahr), the star at the bend of the Big Dipper's handle, is really a double star. Mizar is so far away that without a telescope, the second star is very hard to see. Most other double stars look like single stars unless you look at them through a telescope.

How can the stars help you if you are lost at night?

One very important star can help you—the North Star. There are no South, West, or East stars—in spite of what Lucy says. You can find the North Star easily. The two stars in the front of the Big Dipper point to it.

If you face the North Star, you are facing north. On your right is east. On your left is west. Behind you is south. If your home is south, you turn around and walk away from the North Star.

Which star is nearest to earth?

The sun is the star nearest to earth. It is 93 million miles (150 million kilometers) away. That may not sound very near, but it is close enough to give the earth light and heat.

How hot is the sun?

The outer part of the sun is about 10,000 degrees Fahrenheit (10,000°F., or 5,500°C.). Any metal known on earth would melt at such a high temperature. Most other things on earth would burn up. The inside of the sun is even hotter than the outside. It is almost 30 million degrees Fahrenheit (30,000,000°F., or more than 16,000,000°C.).

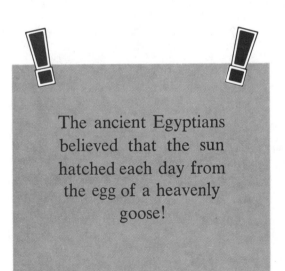

The ancient Egyptians believed that the sun hatched each day from the egg of a heavenly goose!

341

What is the universe?

The word "universe" means everything there is—the sun, the moon, the stars, the earth and all things on it, the other planets, and anything else you can think of. All of space and everything in space is part of the universe. It extends much, much farther than you could see with the most powerful of all telescopes. Most scientists believe that there is an end to the universe. But no one knows where that end is.

What is a galaxy?

A galaxy is a huge group of stars that are close together—close for stars, that is. They are actually many millions of miles apart! Through a telescope, galaxies look like islands. Each one has billions of stars in it. Scientists don't know how many galaxies there are in the universe, but they believe there are millions and millions of them.

All the galaxies in the universe are rushing away from each other at terrific speeds. They will keep on doing so, maybe forever!

What is the Milky Way?

If you look at the night sky, you can often see a glowing band of light. It is what we call the Milky Way. This band is made up of billions of stars. You cannot see the separate stars in the band because they are so far away from the earth.

The glowing band is actually only part of the galaxy that we call the Milky Way Galaxy. This galaxy includes all the separate stars we see in the night sky. These stars are closer to the earth than the band is, so we don't see them all blurred together. Our own star—the sun—and the earth are both part of the Milky Way Galaxy. From far, far out in space, beyond our galaxy, the whole galaxy would appear as one big band of light with a bulge in the middle. From another part of space beyond our galaxy, the Milky Way would appear as a glowing spiral-shaped island.

What is a solar system?

A solar system is a family of ball-shaped objects in space. The family consists of a star, or sun, in the middle with any number of planets traveling around it. The earth is part of a solar system that has a sun in the middle and nine large planets moving around it. The earth is one of these nine planets.

How did our solar system begin?

Scientists don't know for sure. But many think that it formed from a huge pancake-shaped collection of dust in space. For some unknown reason, the "pancake" started to spin. As it spun faster and faster, the center became very hot. It became our sun. At the same time, great blobs of dust broke off from the edges. These collected into nine ball-shaped planets.

The Milky Way from the side.

The Milky Way from above.

What are the planets in our solar system?

There are nine planets in our solar system. The closest to the sun is Mercury. Then come Venus, Earth, Mars, Jupiter, Saturn, Uranus, Neptune, and Pluto. Besides these planets, our solar system also has asteroids (ASS-tuh-roidz) in it.

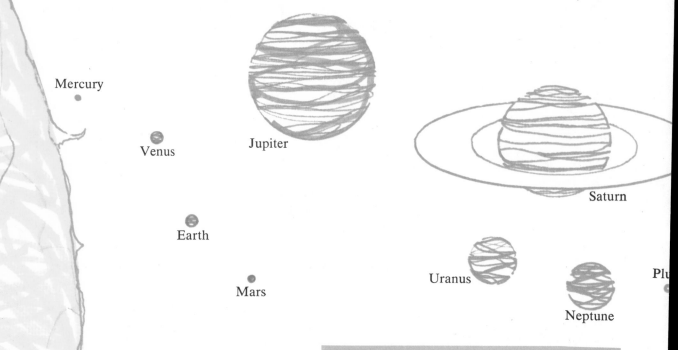

Mercury

Venus

Jupiter

Earth

Mars

Saturn

Uranus

Neptune

Pl

What are asteroids?

Asteroids are tiny planets in our solar system. There are thousands and thousands of them. Most of them travel around the sun between the paths of Mars and Jupiter. The largest is less than 500 miles (800 kilometers) wide. Most asteroids are chunks of rock that are less than one mile wide.

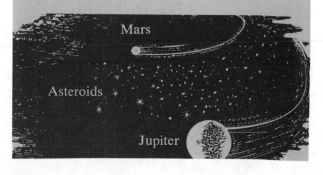

Mars

Asteroids

Jupiter

Can we see any of the nine planets without a telescope?

Yes, we can see six of them—Mercury, Venus, Mars, Jupiter, Saturn, and Uranus. Uranus is very hard to see because it is so far away. Mercury is even harder to see because it is so small. You can usually tell when you're looking at a planet in the night sky because it shines with a bright, steady light. The planets —except for Mercury—usually don't twinkle the way stars do. Whether or not a planet seems to twinkle depends on how far away it is from the earth and where it is in our sky.

The evening star we first see in the night sky is not a star at all.
It is a planet—either Mercury, Venus, Mars, Jupiter, or Saturn!

Are the other planets like the earth?

Not really. Only the earth has air to breathe and water to drink. Mercury is a dead, airless world. During the day it is extremely hot because it is so close to the sun. Venus is covered with thick clouds all the time and is also very hot. Mars is a cold world with hardly any air. Jupiter probably has no solid ground. Scientists believe it may be hot liquid all the way through. The other planets are made mostly of gases and are very cold.

Which of the planets have moons?

Seven planets have moons. Earth has one moon. So does Pluto. Mars has two, and Neptune has two. Uranus has five moons. Saturn has ten. Jupiter has thirteen. Each moon travels in a path around its planet.

How do the planets move?

Each planet moves in two ways at the same time. It moves in a huge egg-shaped path around the sun. This path is called an orbit. Sometimes the planets are closer to one another than at other times. Each planet also spins around on its own axis. A planet's axis is an imaginary line going through the center of the planet. The planet turns around this line. If you were to stick a knitting needle through the center of a ball and spin the ball, it would be spinning on its axis.

Planets orbiting the sun

THAT JUST DOESN'T WORK..

I HAVE TO SLEEP IN THE SAME DIRECTION THAT THE WORLD TURNS

Why don't the planets bump into each other?

The planets can't bump into each other because they travel around the sun in orbits that are millions of miles apart from each other. No planet ever moves out of its orbit.

The planets don't run around bumping into each other because they are polite — unlike some people I know.

347

Does the solar system move?

Yes. The sun and all its planets are traveling around the center of the galaxy. The whole solar system is moving at the speed of 175 miles (280 kilometers) a second!

The huge planet Saturn is so light that it could float on water!

What are Saturn's rings?

The rings are made up of millions of tiny bits of ice and bits of ice-covered dust that orbit Saturn.

Which planet is nearest to the earth?

Venus is the planet nearest to the earth. Much of the time it is about as far from us as we are from the sun.

Which planet is farthest from the earth?

Pluto is the planet farthest from the earth. It is about 40 times farther from the sun than the earth is.

The sun is so far away from Pluto that Pluto never has sunlight—just the darkness of night!

Which is the largest planet?

Jupiter is the largest planet. All the other planets put together could easily fit inside it.

From Pluto, the sun would look like any other star!

Which is the smallest planet?

For many years scientists believed that Mercury was the smallest planet. It is only a little larger than our moon. But now scientists have discovered that faraway Pluto is smaller—even smaller than our moon.

How big is the earth?

It is about 10 times bigger than the planet Mercury. This means that 10 planets the size of Mercury could fit inside the earth. On the other hand, the earth is about 1,300 times smaller than the largest planet, Jupiter. This means that 1,300 planets the size of the earth could fit inside Jupiter.

If you could dig a tunnel through the center of the earth from one side to the other, you would find it measured almost 8,000 miles (12,800 kilometers). That distance is more than 100,000 football fields placed end to end. If you walked clear around the earth, you'd have to walk almost 25,000 miles (40,000 kilometers)—more than 350,000 football fields.

What makes the sun rise?

As Linus said, the sun doesn't rise, the earth turns. The earth is always turning on its axis. If you have a globe at home or in your classroom, you can do an experiment to see why the sun seems to rise. Place a lamp or flashlight so that it shines on the globe. Pretend that the light is sunlight. You can see that the light is hitting only one part of the globe. Now turn the globe slowly. As the globe turns, the part that is lit changes. In the same way, as the earth turns, the part that gets sunlight changes. When the side of the earth you live on doesn't face the sun, you have night. When the earth turns farther around, the part you live on comes into the sunlight. Then the sun seems to rise in the sky. And you have daylight.

Why do we have seasons?

The earth travels around the sun. It takes a year to make the trip. The earth's axis doesn't point straight up and down. So the earth tilts, or tips, a little to one side as it travels. This tilt gives us our four seasons. When the part of the earth you live on tilts towards the sun, you get the most hours of sunlight and the most heat. Then it is summer. When your part of the earth begins to tilt away from the sun, you get less sunlight and less heat. It is fall. When your part of the earth tilts still farther away from the sun, you get even less sunlight and heat. Then it is winter. When your part of the earth begins to tilt closer to the sun again, you get more hours of sunlight and more heat again. Then it is spring.

How fast does the earth travel around the sun?

Scientists have figured out that the earth is racing through space at 66,600 miles (107,200 kilometers) an hour—thousands of times faster than the fastest racing car. During the time it took you to read this answer, the earth probably moved through space more than 300 miles (480 kilometers)!

Why don't you feel the earth moving?

You can't feel the earth moving through space because it moves so smoothly. When you ride in a car, you know you're moving, even if you close your eyes. That is because the ride is bumpy. When you are on a jet plane and you close your eyes, most of the time you cannot tell that the plane is moving. That is because the ride is quite smooth. The movement of the earth through space is even smoother. And so you cannot feel it at all.

Fall

Summer

Winter

Spring

Why does the moon shine?

The moon does not shine with its own light. It has no light to give out. The moon reflects, or sends back, some of the light rays that come to it from the sun. Those light rays reach the earth—and your eyes. On a sunny day, a friend's eyeglasses reflect light in much the way the moon does. The glare you see on them isn't their own light. Instead they are reflecting the sun's rays to your eyes.

Just as the sun shines on some part of the earth at all times, the sun shines on some part of the moon at all times. The moon is always reflecting some sunlight, but you cannot always see it. During the day, the sun shines on the part of the earth where you live. The sun's light is brighter than the moon's light. So the sunlight usually hides the moon from your sight. At night no sunlight hides the moon, so you can see it "shining."

The sun's rays bounce not only off the moon, but off the earth. If you were out in space, you would see the earth shining more brightly than the moon!

How far from the earth is the moon?

The moon is about 239,000 miles (384,000 kilometers) away from the earth. How far is that?—farther than a rope would extend if it were long enough to be wrapped around the earth nine times.

Why can't we see the back of the moon?

Just as the earth moves in two different ways, the moon also moves in two different ways. It turns on its axis and it travels in its orbit around the earth. The moon takes 27 days, 7 hours, and 43 minutes to turn around once on its axis. The moon takes just about the same amount of time to travel once around the earth. This means that the moon always keeps the same side facing the earth. From the earth you never see the back of the moon.

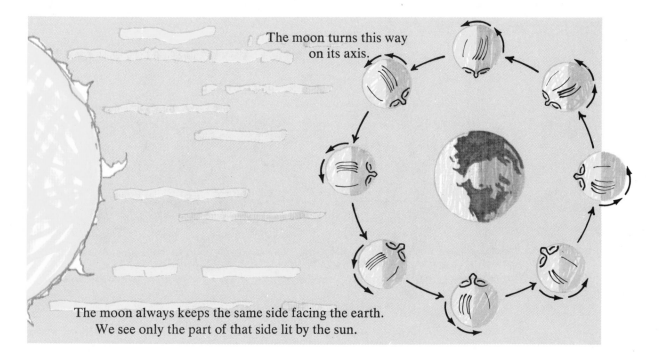

The moon turns this way on its axis.

The moon always keeps the same side facing the earth. We see only the part of that side lit by the sun.

Why doesn't the moon always look round?

The moon has no light of its own. Light comes to it from the sun, just as light comes to the earth from the sun. A part of the moon is always turned to the sun and a part of it is always turned away from the sun. One part is as dark as night. The other part is as bright as day. We see the moon only when some of the lighted part is turned toward the earth.

As the moon travels around the earth, it always keeps the same side facing the earth. But we can't always see all of that side because different amounts of it are lit by the sun during different days of the month. So sometimes we see just a sliver. Sometimes we see a half moon, and sometimes we see a full moon. The picture on this page should help you understand how this happens.

KEEP MOVING, SCOUTS, AND WE'LL GET HOME BY THE LIGHT OF THE MOON...

What causes an eclipse of the moon?

When light shines on anything, that thing casts a shadow. The earth is no exception. When the sun shines on the earth, the earth has a shadow on its opposite side. An eclipse of the moon happens when the moon moves behind the earth and into the earth's shadow. Because the moon is in this shadow, most of the sun's light cannot hit the moon. There is scarcely any light to bounce off the moon, so you can hardly see it. What you do see of the moon looks reddish. When the moon comes out from the earth's shadow, it shines again with full light from the sun. The eclipse is over.

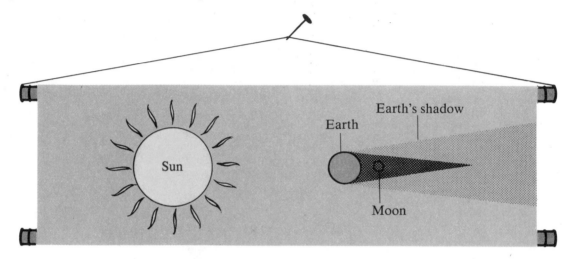

There are at least two eclipses every year.
But there can never be more than seven!

354

What causes an eclipse of the sun?

An eclipse of the sun happens when the moon moves directly in front of the sun. The moon's shadow is cast on the earth. The sun's light is blotted out at certain places on the earth by the moon. If you are in one of these shadowy places, you see an eclipse of the sun. You see the round disk of the moon passing across the face of the sun.

Because looking straight at the sun can damage your eyes, you should never do it—even during an eclipse.

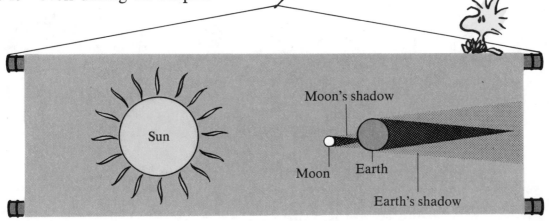

What's the difference between a "total eclipse" and a "partial eclipse"?

"Total eclipse" means that the whole sun or the whole moon is blocked from view. "Partial eclipse" means that only a part of the moon or the sun is blocked out.

Total eclipse of the sun.

Partial eclipse of the sun.

Why can't a football fall off the earth?

A football, or any other thing, cannot fall off the earth because it is always pulled to the earth by gravity. Gravity is a force—a tremendous pull—that draws all things on the earth down toward the earth's center.

Is the earth the only planet with gravity?

No. Each planet has gravity. That means that Mars pulls things toward its center. Pluto pulls things toward its center. So do Saturn, Jupiter, and all the others. In fact, everything in the universe has gravity—even a pencil and a grain of sand. Of course, the bigger the object is, the stronger its pull. A tiny asteroid doesn't have much gravity. Stars have the greatest gravity because they are bigger than any other objects in the universe. A spaceship at equal distance from a star and an asteroid would be pulled toward the star. The strong pull of our sun keeps the planets in their orbits around it.

What is a comet?

A comet is a large ball of glowing gases, dust, and ice. It travels in a long cigar-shaped orbit around the sun. Comets that can be seen without a telescope always have tails of glowing gases streaming out behind them. A comet's tail always points away from the sun because the strong energy coming from the sun blows the glowing gases backward off the comet.

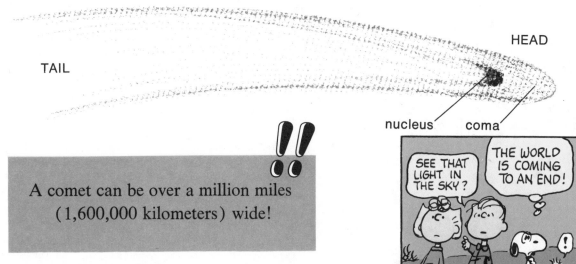

TAIL

HEAD

nucleus   coma

A comet can be over a million miles (1,600,000 kilometers) wide!

Why are some people afraid of comets?

Snoopy and Woodstock may be afraid of comets, but most people today aren't. Long, long ago, however, comets were very frightening. People believed that a comet's sudden appearance in the sky meant that bad things were going to happen—sickness, war, poor crops, floods, the death of a ruler, or even the end of the world. They were afraid that the comet would crash into the earth and destroy it. In 1910, the earth did pass through the tail of a comet called Halley's Comet. Nothing seemed to happen because of it. However, a head-on collision between the earth and a comet could be very dangerous. Happily, no comet except Halley's has come very close to the earth. So we haven't had any problem yet, and we probably never will.

357

What is a shooting star?

Shooting stars aren't stars at all. They are the bright streaks of light you can see passing quickly through the dark sky on a clear night. Scientists call these streaks meteors (MEE-tee-urz). A meteor can be caused by a bit of dust or a very tiny rock that has been traveling at a terrific speed through space. When the bit of rock or dust hits the earth's blanket of air, its movement heats the air. The air gets so hot that it glows. The long trail of glowing air is the shooting "star" we see in the night sky. A very brilliant meteor that leaves a shining trail as it streaks across the sky is called a fireball. Its trail lasts for a few minutes.

What's the difference between a meteor and a meteorite?

A meteor is a streak, or flash, of light. You see it when a bit of rock or dust from outer space enters the earth's air at high speed. Usually the rock or dust burns up before it hits the ground. A meteorite (MEE-tee-ur-ite) is any piece of rock from space that doesn't burn up. It falls through the earth's blanket of air and lands on the ground.

What is a meteor shower?

A meteor shower happens when many, many meteors fall from the same place in the sky. A meteor shower can last for hours or even a few days. Scientists think the meteors of a meteor shower are caused by millions of tiny pieces of a broken-up comet. These pieces crash into the earth's air and burn up in it.

QUICK, QUICK... CATCH A FALLING STAR CHARLIE BROWN...

During a 20-minute meteor shower in 1966, people counted 2,300 meteors each minute!

359

What is astrology?

People who believe in astrology think that the stars and planets have a lot to do with their lives. Since everything in the universe keeps moving, the planets and stars are in different places on different days of the year. People who believe in astrology think that the position of certain planets and stars influence their lives in special ways, depending on when and where they were born. They say that the positions of the planets and stars tell them what kind of people they are, how they can live better lives, and what will happen in the future. The advice an astrology expert gives about the future is called a horoscope (HAWR-uh-scope). Most scientists do not believe in astrology and horoscopes.

What is a plant?

Anything that is alive and isn't an animal is a plant. Unlike animals, most plants stay in one place. They don't walk, swim, or fly. Most plants have green leaves. In them is the chemical chlorophyll (KLAWR-uh-fill), which gives the leaves their green color. A few plants with chlorophyll don't have green leaves. They have red, purple, or brown leaves instead. Any plant that has chlorophyll is called a "green plant" even if no green shows on its leaves. Green plants make their own food. Other plants don't. Instead, they take their food from animals or other plants. Non-green plants may be completely brown, white, or even red.

How many kinds of plants are there?

There are about 350,000 different kinds of plants on earth. They come in all sizes. Some are so tiny that you can see them only under a microscope. Others are so large that they tower hundreds of feet above the ground. In fact, the tallest living thing is a plant—the giant redwood tree. It can grow as high as 300 feet (90 meters).

Plants have many different shapes, too. A blade of grass is long and skinny. A palm tree has large leaves and a long trunk. A cabbage is round and leafy. A mushroom is shaped like an umbrella. A cactus is usually narrow with sharp spines.

"I THINK THAT I SHALL NEVER SEE A POEM AS LOVELY AS A...PALM...??"

SIGH!

How long have plants been on earth?

Plants have been on earth for more than three billion (3,000,000,000) years and possibly as long as four billion (4,000,000,000) years. The first plants were tiny water plants—the kind you can see only under a microscope. They were on earth many millions of years before dinosaurs. In fact, they were here long before any animals.

Is a flower a plant?

According to plant scientists, a flower is not a whole plant, but just one part of a plant—the blossom. Not all plants have blossoms. Those that do are called flowering plants.

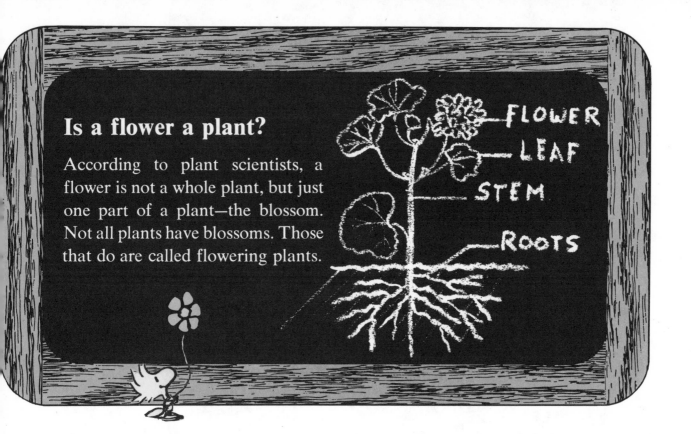

FLOWER
LEAF
STEM
ROOTS

Why do green plants need leaves, roots, flowers, stems?

A green plant makes its own food. Most of the food is made in its leaves.

Roots hold a plant firmly in the ground so that it does not fall over or blow away. The roots also take water and minerals out of the soil. The plant needs these things to live. Sometimes roots store some of the food that the leaves make.

The flowers are the parts of the plant where seeds can form. The seeds will someday become new plants.

The stems hold up the leaves and flowers. They have tubes in them that carry liquids up and down the plant. Some of the tubes bring water mixed with minerals from the roots to the leaves and flowers. Other tubes carry liquid food away from the leaves to the rest of the plant. We call the two liquids sap.

The largest flowering plant growing on earth today is a Chinese wisteria (wih-STEER-ee-uh). It has branches 500 feet (150 meters) long, and it weighs as much as 50 elephants!

363

How do leaves make food?

The leaves of a green plant are like little food factories. Inside them is the chemical chlorophyll, which makes the leaves green. The leaves need the chlorophyll in order to make food. When the sun shines on the chlorophyll, each leaf factory goes to work.

The factory uses two things to make food. It uses water that has come up from the soil, through the roots and stems. It uses a gas called carbon dioxide (die-OCK-side) that has come from the air, through tiny openings in the leaf. From the water and carbon dioxide it makes sugar, which is the plant's food. At the same time, the factory makes a gas called oxygen (OCK-suh-jin). Most of this oxygen goes into the air.

The food factory works only when the sun is shining. When the sun goes down, the factory stops. Without sunlight (or an electric plant-light) green plants cannot make food and they die.

Why do leaves of house plants turn toward the window?

If you let a green plant stand on your window sill, its leaves will turn toward the window. This may happen after a few hours or a few days. If you turn the plant around, the leaves will again move and face the window. Why? Because light is coming in the window, and green plants need all the light they can get to make food. The leaves are reaching for the light.

Outdoors, most green plants have bright light all around them, so their leaves don't turn. But they, too, would turn if light reached them from only one direction.

A pine needle is really a leaf!

What is a carrot?

A carrot is the root of a carrot plant. This root is filled with stored food. When the leaves of a plant make food, the plant uses some of it for energy to grow. Extra food is stored in the plant's roots, stems, fruit, seeds, and even in its leaves. A carrot plant stores most of its extra food in its root. When you eat a carrot, you are eating this stored food.

Carrots are not the only roots you may eat. Beets are roots. So are sweet potatoes. Like carrots, they are filled with stored food. Celery stalks are stems that have food stored in them. So are asparagus stalks. Lettuce, cabbage, and spinach are leaves with a little food stored in them. Apples, peaches, and grapes are the fruits of plants. Peas, lima beans, and corn kernels are all seeds. They, too, hold stored food.

What is a fruit?

We usually think of a fruit as a sweet and juicy food. But plant scientists think of fruits in another way. To them a fruit is the seed or seeds of any plant together with the fleshy parts around them. For example, string beans, eggplants, and tomatoes all have seeds inside them. So to a plant scientist they are fruits, although most of us would call them vegetables. Apples, oranges, cherries, and bananas are fruits both to us and to the plant scientists.

What do plant scientists mean by the word "vegetables"? They never use that word. They talk about roots, stems, and leaves—but not about vegetables.

Do all plants make their own food?

No. Only green plants—plants that have chlorophyll—can make their own food. All other plants cannot. A plant that doesn't make food is called a fungus. More than one of these plants are called fungi (FUN-jI). Some fungi take their food from dead wood or from soil that has rotting plants in it. Others take their food from living plants and sometimes from living animals. Some fungi even live on people. A rash called athlete's foot is caused by fungi living on a person's skin.

The fungi you probably know the best are mushrooms. These usually grow in areas where there is very little sun. Because mushrooms don't make their own food, they don't need sunlight.

What's the difference between a mushroom and a toadstool?

Toadstools are poisonous mushrooms. Toadstools got their name because people used to think that poisonous toads sat on them. Unless you are an expert, it is almost impossible to tell a poisonous mushroom from a good one. If you just want to touch mushrooms, they all are safe. But if you want to eat them, you'd better buy your mushrooms at the supermarket.

OH...OOO
I THINK I'VE BEEN
ZAPPED BY A
TOADSTOOL!

What makes bread get moldy?

All around us in the air are tiny black and green specks called spores. They are too small for us to see without a microscope. But they are there all the same. These spores are like seeds for certain plants called molds. Molds are fungi and do not make their own food. They live off some of the foods we like to eat. Bread is one of them. When bread is moldy, you know that bread-mold spores have landed there. The spores have grown into fuzzy-looking mold plants which are eating the bread.

The medicine penicillin comes from a mold that is very much like bread mold!

Why do lakes and rivers sometimes turn green and slimy?

Dirty water from toilets is often dumped into lakes and rivers. And fertilizers, which make farmers' crops grow better, are often washed by rain into lakes and rivers, too. In these same waters live tiny green plants called algae (AL-jee). Both the fertilizers and the human wastes make the algae grow faster. They grow so fast that they may cover the whole top of a lake or a large part of a river. They make the water look green and slimy. Any fish living in this slimy water will die.

What is the crust you sometimes see on rocks?

The gray or colored crusts that you see on rocks are plants called lichens (LIKE-inz). You can find them growing not only on rocks, but also on tree bark and even on sand. You can find lichens in hot deserts and on cold high mountains where no other plants can grow.

How can lichens live in these harsh places? Lichens are made up of two kinds of tiny plants living together—algae and fungi. Lichens don't need wet soil to get water because both the algae and fungi can take water out of the air. The algae, which are green plants, also made food for the lichens. No one is sure what else the fungi do. But when living together as lichens, the algae and fungi can survive in places where they could not live alone.

369

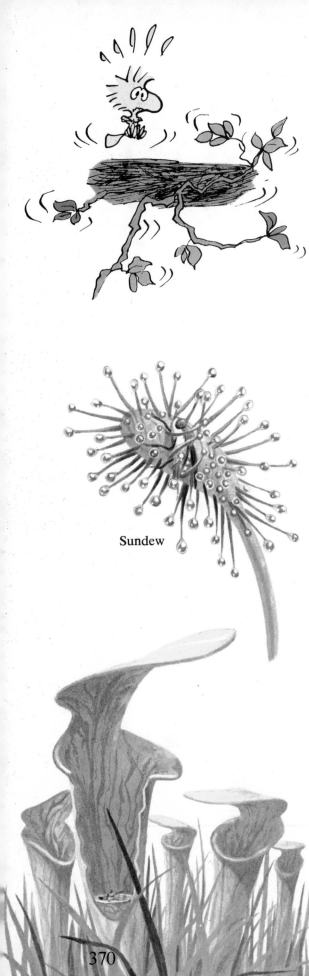

Venus's-flytrap

Sundew

Pitcher plant

Do any plants eat animals?

Yes, there are plants that eat insects and one that can eat small birds and mice! Three of the animal-eating plants are the pitcher plant, the sundew, and Venus's-flytrap.

The pitcher plant has leaves that are shaped like pitchers or vases. The pitchers have a sweet smell that attracts insects. At the bottom of each pitcher is water. If an insect falls inside, it drowns. The plant then digests the insect in much the same way that your body digests food. One kind of pitcher plant has pitchers so large that small birds and mice sometimes fall inside and are digested.

The sundew has leaves covered with many hairs. Each hair has a drop of sticky liquid at its tip. In the sunlight, these drops of liquid shine like dew. They also smell sweet. Insects are attracted to the plant. When an insect lands on a leaf, it gets caught in the sticky drops. The hairs bend over the insect and hold it down. Then the plant digests it.

Venus's-flytrap is well named. Each leaf can fold along the center and close up like a trap. On each leaf are little hairs. When an insect lands on these hairs, the two parts of the leaf close, trapping the insect inside. After the insect is digested, the leaf opens again.

Even though the pitcher plant, the sundew, and Venus's-flytrap eat insects, they are all green plants and make their own food as well. However, certain minerals are missing from the soil in which they live. They get these minerals from the insects they eat.

370

Why do bees fly around flowers?

Bees go to flowers to get nectar and pollen. They use the nectar, a sweet liquid found inside many flowers, to make honey. They take home the pollen, a powder in the flowers, to eat and to feed to their young.

SOMEHOW I FEEL RIDICULOUS EXPLAINING THE BIRDS AND BEES TO WOODSTOCK!

Do bees do anything for flowers?

Yes, bees help flowers make seeds. Most flowers can't make seeds unless they get some pollen from another flower of the same kind. Bees bring this other pollen to the flowers when the bees fly around gathering food. Here's how it works:

Bees go to only one kind of flower at a time. When a bee lands on a flower, it brushes against tiny spikes called stamens (STAY-minz). On the stamens is pollen. Some pollen brushes off onto the bee's furry body. Then, when the bee lands on another flower, some of this pollen falls off its body.

Inside flowers is another spike called a pistil. When the pollen from one flower lands on the pistil of another flower of the same kind, we say the plant has been pollinated. Now seeds can start to grow. Seeds will not grow unless the flower is pollinated. From the seeds will come new plants someday.

Bees are not the only things that pollinate flowers. Sometimes the wind carries pollen from one plant to another. Often butterflies, moths, wasps, flies, beetles, birds, and even bats do the job. They go to the flowers looking for nectar. The flowers attract the creatures with special smells or colors.

371

Do all flowers smell sweet?

No. Only flowers that attract bees, butterflies, moths, and some other insects have a sweet smell. Flowers that attract birds do not. Birds have a poor sense of smell, but they are attracted to bright colors. "Bird" flowers are usually bright red or orange. They also hold a lot of nectar. Only birds that like nectar pollinate flowers.

Flowers that are pollinated by flies have a smell, but not a sweet one. These "fly" flowers smell like rotting meat! "Bat" flowers also smell bad to people, but bats like the smell. Flowers that are pollinated by the wind have no smell at all. They don't have any nectar either, and they have very dull colors. These flowers don't need to attract anyone. They are often small and hard to notice.

Why does the dandelion turn white and fluffy?

The dandelion flower turns white and fluffy so that the wind can carry away its seeds. After a dandelion flower has been pollinated, seeds begin to grow inside it. When the seeds are ripe, the yellow petals fall off the flower. Fluffy white hairs sprout at the top of each seed. The wind catches the fluff and carries the seed away from the plant. After a while, the seed lands on the ground. If the seed gets pushed into the ground by an animal or rain, the seed will grow into a new plant.

Because dandelion seeds are spread by the wind, new dandelions can grow in many places. If all the dandelion seeds simply dropped to the ground right under the plant, the seeds would be too close together. When they sprouted, the new plants would not have room to grow well.

Are all seeds spread by the wind?

No. All seeds are spread in some way, but not all by the wind. The wind spreads seeds that are tiny or fluffy and can easily float in the air. It also spreads seeds that have "wings," such as maple seeds.

Water sometimes spreads these winged seeds, too. Any seeds that are able to float can be spread by water. Such seeds may travel long distances before they reach land again. Animals also spread seeds. Some seeds have sharp hooks that get stuck to an animal's fur and fall off later. Burrs, or "stickers," are seeds of this kind. Some birds and other animals eat fruits. They may carry off the fruits and then drop the seeds far away.

One kind of daisy is pollinated by a snail!

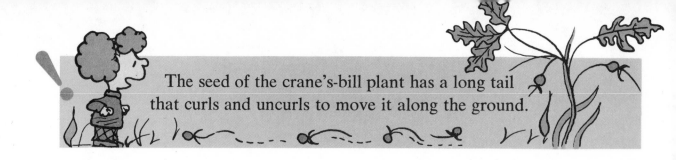

How does a seed become a new plant?

If you have ever eaten a sunflower seed, you have had to crack open the hard shell outside to get to the soft part inside. Some of this soft part is the beginning of a new sunflower plant. It is called an embryo (EM-bree-oh). The rest of the soft part is stored food. Inside every seed is an embryo with stored food. The hard shell protects the embryo.

The embryo forms while the seed is still on the plant. Once it is formed, it stops growing for a while. But it has enough stored food around it to give it energy to grow again. It will grow as soon as it is in the right soil with the right temperature and the right amount of water. Then the embryo will sprout roots and a stem. It will grow leaves and start making its own food. It will become a whole plant and make seeds of its own.

What is a pine cone?

When a pine cone first grows, it is a kind of flower. Later on it acts as the tree's fruit because it holds seeds. When the pine cone is still a flower, it is covered with soft scales. After it has been pollinated by the wind, seeds begin to grow inside it. The scales harden and protect the seeds. The seeds may grow inside the hardened cone for several years. But at last they become ready to fall to the ground or to be blown away by the wind.

Other trees that are related to the pine also have cones. Firs, spruces, and cedars are some of these trees.

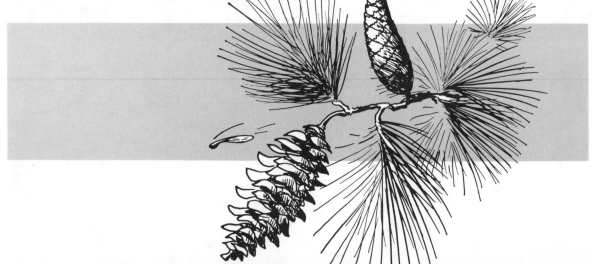

Do all new plants come from seeds?

Plants that have flowers come from seeds. But other plants start in other ways.

Some very tiny plants—the kind you can see only under a microscope—make new plants simply by dividing in half. Each part becomes a whole new plant. Other microscopic plants grow "buds." These buds have nothing to do with flowers. They are whole plants, smaller than their parent, but otherwise just like it. A bud stays attached to the parent until it grows to nearly full size. Then it splits off from the parent plant and lives on its own.

Some algae and fungi grow tiny specks, called spores, instead of seeds. From each spore can come a new plant. Look under the umbrella of a ripe mushroom and you will see the mushroom spores.

Ferns also produce spores. These are inside small brown cases that you can see lined up on the underside of the fern's leaves. When the spores are ripe, the cases burst open and the spores are scattered.

> I THINK PLANTS GIVE AN OFFICE A LITTLE CLASS.

THE DOCTOR IS **WAY OUT**

Ferns come out of the ground all curled up, and then they unfold!

I HEARD YOUR FAMILY IS GOING AWAY FOR THE WEEKEND.

ASK YOUR MOM IF SHE'D LIKE TO HIRE A PLANT SITTER.

WHAT DO YOU KNOW ABOUT PLANT SITTING?

ENOUGH!

WHAT WOULD YOU DO IF THEY CRIED?

Why do people put plant stems in water?

People put flower stems in water to make the flowers last longer. People put leafy stems in water to grow roots. Once roots have grown, the stems can be planted in soil. Then they will grow into full-sized plants. The plants that can grow roots on their stems also have seeds. But seeds may take a few weeks or months to begin growing. Some stems can grow roots in water in just a few days. You can grow roots on the stems of many plants, including begonias, ivy, and coleus (KOE-lee-us) by putting them in water.

HOW ABOUT THAT, CHUCK!

WOW!

Are there any other quick ways to grow plants?

Yes. Sometimes stems with leaves on them will grow if you simply put them in soil and water them well. You can grow a pineapple plant from the top of a pineapple this way. Cut off the leafy top, strip some of the lower leaves off the stem, and stick the stem in a pot of soil. With the right amount of water and sunlight, the stem will grow into a whole new pineapple plant.

Set a sweet potato in a jar of water so that some of the sweet potato sticks out above the jar. Roots will grow from the part under water. Long stems with leaves will grow out of the dry top part.

You can also grow many new potato plants from one white potato. On each potato you will see little dark bumps. These are called eyes. Cut up a potato so that each piece has one eye. If you plant the pieces in soil, a new plant will grow from each eye.

What is a tulip bulb?

A tulip bulb is a special underground part of the tulip plant. On the outside of the bulb is a brown skinlike covering. Inside is the bud of a flower and a short stem with thick leaves packed tightly around it. The leaves hold extra food for the plant so that it can live through the winter and grow again in the spring.

In spring the tulip leaves, stem, and bud come out of the bulb. They push above the ground. The tulip bud grows and opens. After the flower is pollinated, the flower petals fall off the stem, and seeds fall to the ground. But the leaves are still on the plant, and they are still making food. The food is stored in the underground bulb. After the summer, the leaves and stem fall off the plant. Above the ground, the plant cannot be seen. But underground there is still a living plant in the form of the roots and bulb. In the fall a new stem, bud, and leaves form in the bulb. The plant stays underground all winter, using the stored food. When the weather gets warm again, the bulb sends up the new leaves, stem, and bud. The whole story repeats itself year after year.

Although most people plant bulbs to get tulip flowers, you can also grow tulips from their seeds. But if you do, you will have to wait three to seven years before you get any flowers.

377

What is a weed?

A weed is any plant that grows where people don't want it to grow. For example, when farmers are growing potatoes, they don't want any other plants growing in the same soil. Other plants will take minerals and water from the soil that the farmers want their potatoes to have. So they call any other plant a weed. Farmers spray their potato fields with special chemicals to keep weeds from growing. They dig up any weeds that do sprout there. Plants whose seeds scatter easily are often called weeds because they come up in many unwanted places.

How can you tell how old a tree is?

When a tree is cut down, you can usually see rings on the tree stump. The rings show how long the tree was growing. Twice each year, a tree grows some new wood. The new wood forms a ring around the old wood of the tree trunk. In the spring, the tree grows a light-colored ring. In the summer, it grows a dark-colored ring. So if a tree stump has 24 rings, you know that the tree was 12 years old when it was cut down. If the stump has 200 rings, you know that the tree was 100 years old.

HERE'S THE WORL FAMOUS BEAGLE SC TEACHING HIS TROO HOW TO TELL THE A(OF A TREE.

Some bristlecone pine trees have lived nearly 5,000 years.

378

Why do leaves turn colors in the fall?

Leaves have many colors in them—green, red, orange, yellow. But during the spring and summer, there is much more green than any other color. The green comes from the chlorophyll which leaves use in making food. The leaves have so much chlorophyll that you usually can't see the other colors. But in the fall, before cold weather sets in, many trees stop making food. At the same time they stop making chlorophyll. When the chlorophyll disappears, you can see the other colors in the leaves.

Why do leaves fall off the trees in the fall?

During warm weather, the leaves of a tree are always giving off tiny drops of water. At the same time, the tree's roots are taking in more water so that the tree does not dry out. But during cold weather, the ground freezes. The roots cannot get any water. If the leaves kept on giving off water, the tree would dry up and die.

In the fall, a layer of cork grows at the bottom of each leaf stem. It blocks water from flowing into the leaf. The leaf dries up. It is easily taken off the tree by the wind. And so it falls to the ground.

379

Why is a cactus covered with spines?

The thin, sharp spines of a cactus protect it in two ways. First, they keep the cactus from losing a lot of water. Plants are always losing water through their leaves. Plants that have large leaves may lose a few gallons a day. A cactus lives in the desert where there is very little water. If it lost much water, it would quickly die. So, instead of large leaves, the cactus has small spines. They are so thin that little water can escape through them.

The spines also protect the cactus by being sharp. A cactus stores a lot of water in its stem. Desert animals might break open the cactus to get this water, but the sharp spines keep the animals away.

Why does poison ivy make you itch?

Poison ivy

The poison ivy plant has an oil on it. This oil can make your skin break out in an itchy rash. If you know what a poison ivy plant looks like, you can keep from touching it.

Poison ivy can grow as a bush or as a vine that climbs on other trees. The plant's leaves are each made up of three leaflets (three leaves on one stem). They are shiny and green in spring and summer. They turn a bright red in the fall.

Does a four-leaf clover really bring good luck?

You are lucky to find a four-leaf clover because most clover plants have only three leaves on each stem. But there is no way that a four-leaf clover or any other plant can bring you good luck.

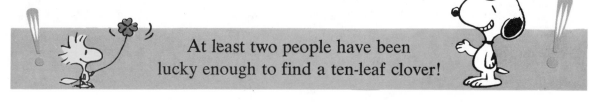

At least two people have been lucky enough to find a ten-leaf clover!

What are tree surgeons?

Tree surgeons act as doctors for trees. They take care of trees, keeping them healthy and healing them when they are hurt or sick. Tree surgeons cut back branches that have gotten too long, spray chemicals on insects or fungi living in a tree, paint a protective coating over cuts, and take off dead wood. In a way, tree surgeons are also like dentists because they fill in cavities, or holes, in trees. The holes are made by fungi, insects, or woodpeckers.

Do plants feel pain when they are cut?

No. Animals feel pain because they have nerves inside them that carry messages of pain to their brains. But plants don't have nerves or brains. So they can't feel pain the way we do.

Do plants grow better if you talk to them?

No one knows for sure. Many scientists think that sound can affect plants. Soft, quiet music seems to help them grow better. Loud music with drums seems to kill them. But plants can't understand words, so saying nice things to a plant should not affect it. Still, some scientists claim that plants react to the feelings in people's words—and even in their thoughts. They say that plants grow better if you think nice thoughts and that they "faint" or even die if you think nasty thoughts. But other scientists don't believe that these things are true. Many people have done experiments to find out if they are. So far everyone seems to have come up with a different answer.

Which foods that people eat come from plants?

Fruits and vegetables, of course, come from plants. But they are not the only foods that do. Coffee comes from the seeds of the coffee plant. Chocolate comes from the seeds of the cacao (kuh-KAY-O) plant. Honey is made by bees from the nectar in flowers. Sugar can be made from two different plants —sugar cane or sugar beets. Sweet maple syrup comes from the sap of the sugar-maple tree. Wine is made from grapes. Meat and milk don't come from plants—but they're from animals that eat plants. In fact, one way or another, all our food comes from plants—except salt and chemical food made in factories.

Cacao tree

382

What would happen if all the plants on earth died?

If all the plants on earth died, so would all the animals—including people. We need plants in order to live. When green plants make food, they give off oxygen. This is a gas that all animals must breathe in order to stay alive. Without plants, animals would have no oxygen to breathe and would die.

Animals also depend on plants for their food. All animals eat either plants or plant-eating animals. Without plants there would be almost no food on earth!

IT SAYS HERE THAT "WITHOUT PLANTS THERE WOULD BE ALMOST NO FOOD ON EARTH." ...THAT KIND OF TALK GIVES MY STOMACH A HEADACHE.

FLOATING OUT TO SEA ON A PITCHER'S MOUND... I CAN'T BELIEVE IT!

CHARLIE BROWN'S IN TROUBLE, SNOOPY... WE SHOULD DO SOMETHING...

THAT'S TRUE!

IF HE'S NOT GOING TO BE AROUND TO FEED ME ANY MORE, MAYBE I SHOULD PLANT A GARDEN...

LET'S SEE, I COULD PUT SOME TOMATOES HERE, AND SOME CORN OVER THERE AND MAYBE SOME RADISHES HERE..

What things that we use every day come from plants?

Flax

Cotton

Everything made of wood comes from the trunk of a tree. Houses, fences, furniture, and paper are all made of wood.

From the sap of the rubber tree comes rubber. Tires, shoe heels, rubber bands, rubber balls, diving suits, and many toys are made of rubber.

Cotton cloth is made from the cotton plant. Linen cloth is made from the flax plant. From cotton and linen cloth we make clothes, curtains, towels, and sheets.

Many medicines come from plants. Penicillin comes from a mold. Quinine, used to treat the disease called malaria, comes from the bark of the cinchona (sin-KOE-nuh) tree. Digitalis (dij-ih-TAL-iss), used to treat weak hearts, is made from dried leaves of the foxglove plant.

What is recycled paper?

Recycled paper is new paper made out of old. Most paper is made from the trunk of a tree. Each year people use more and more things made of paper—towels, napkins, plates, cups, books, magazines, newspapers, and stationery. To get all this paper, trees are cut down every day. New trees are often planted in their place, but new trees take a long time to grow. In order to save some trees we need to use less paper or reuse old paper.

Scientists have invented a way to reuse paper. We call this "recycling" the paper. Here is how it is done. Old newspaper is first shredded into little pieces. Then it is put into chemicals that clean it and make it soft and mushy. The mushy paper is mixed with water, flattened, and spread to dry. When it is dry, it is fresh, clean paper—recycled paper.

Did You Know That...

Scientists who study the universe are called astronomers (uh-STRON-uh-merz). Many of the things they learn about the stars and planets turn out to be useful here on earth. Astronomers made many of the earliest discoveries about the laws of motion and gravity. They invented the lenses that made telescopes and microscopes possible. Astronomers developed many ways to use mathematics to find things out. Their work has also made time keeping and navigation more accurate. Astronomers keep bringing us new knowledge about our universe.

The sun is the brightest star in our sky. The next brightest is Sirius the Dog Star. It has that name because it is in the group of stars called Canis Major. That means Great Dog.

Greenhouses are special buildings that are designed to give plants the special conditions they need in order to grow. Most greenhouses have glass roofs and walls to let in plenty of light. Many can be heated and cooled to keep the temperatures just right for the plants. Because the temperature and water supply can be different in each room of a greenhouse, a cactus garden can grow next door to a jungle.

Interior of greenhouse

Light travels very quickly—186,000 miles a second. Even at this speed, it still takes the sun's light eight minutes to reach the earth. But that's not so long when you consider the rest of the universe. Proxima Centauri is the next closest star to earth. It takes four years for its light to reach earth.

Each day the earth turns completely around one time. It turns from the west to the east. That is why the sun "rises" in the east and "sets" in the west. Many of the planets also spin from west to east. But Venus and Uranus are different—they spin from east to west. Scientists have not been able to explain why this happens.

The petals of most flowers open in the morning and close in the evening. But the moon cactus has blossoms that open only at night.

Moon cactus

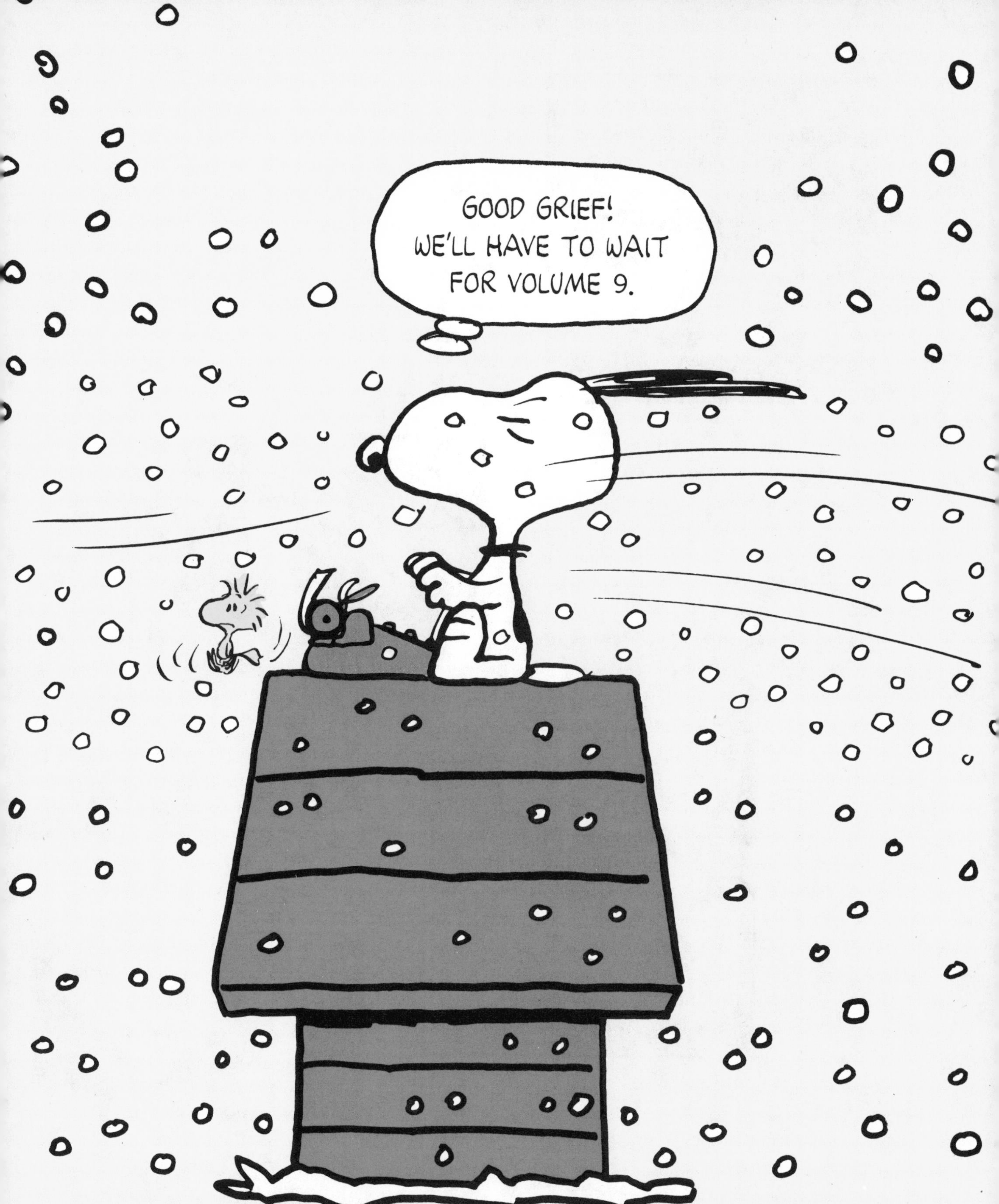
GOOD GRIEF! WE'LL HAVE TO WAIT FOR VOLUME 9.